On Vital Reserves

On Vital Reserves

With a modern Introduction
by STEPHEN VICCHIO

Christian Classics, Inc.

P.O. BOX 30 • WESTMINSTER, MD 21157

"The Energies of Men" was first published in *The Philosophical Review* in 1907 and republished later in the same year in the *American Magazine* under the title, "The Powers of Men." "The Gospel of Relaxation" was published by Henry Holt and Co. in 1899.

ISBN: 0-87061-151-8

Printed in the United States of America

Contents

A Modern Introduction

by STEPHEN JOHN VICCHIO
author of A Careful Disorder

Some Comments on the Life, Thought and Influence of William James

> The life of William James was widely spread both in its roots and its branches. It took its nourishment from many sources, grew in many directions, and bore a great variety of fruits. It was richly fertilized and abundantly fertile.
> —RALPH BARTON PERRY

I

There are sometimes single moments in each of our lives when, in looking back, we may say without hesitation, "Yes, my life began a profound change there." One of those moments for William James, the great American psychologist and philosopher, came on April 30, 1870. After reading an essay by the 19th century French philosopher, Charles Renouvier, James made the following entry in his diary:

> I think yesterday was a crisis in my life. I finished the first part of Renouvier's second essay and saw no reason why his definition of free will—'the sustaining of

a thought because I choose to' when I
might have other thoughts—need be the
definition of an illusion. My first act of
free will shall be to believe in free will.[1]

Before that day, James had suffered a life full
of anxiety, fear, and self-deprecation. He was
born in New York City on January 11, 1842, to a
well-to-do second generation American family.
In keeping with his father, Henry James Sr.'s
theories about education and the proper conduct
of life, William and Henry Jr., the great American
novelist, received irregular schooling, first at
home and then throughout western Europe.

The father of Henry Sr. was the first William
James, an Irishman who immigrated to America in the last decade of the 18th century with no
money and no real employable skills. Through
shrewd judgement, parsimony, and a Calvinist
faith, he became a millionaire banker and en-
trepreneur. But the elder William James was an
insecure and distant man, so active in his finan-
cial and civic affairs that he had little time for his
wife and children.

Henry Sr. rejected both his father's Presbyterian-
ism and his cold but stern methods of child rear-
ing. Indeed, it might be said that Henry made
the happiness of his family his life's work. It
could also be said, however, that he was not al-

ways so successful in that work. Henry Sr., perhaps in a reaction to his unhappy childhood, tended to be overprotective and indulgent to a fault. The consequences were probably felt most acutely by the youngest child, Alice, and the oldest, William.

In 1865, after a brief study of art in Newport, Rhode Island, under the painter William Morris Hunt, and an even briefer stay at the Harvard Medical School, William James accompanied the Swiss-American naturalist, Louis Agassiz, on an expedition up the Brazilian Amazon. Several months later, James returned to the states complaining of severe lower back pain. The following year was spent in Germany dividing his time among medical classes, lectures in psychology and philosophy, and visits to the mineral baths at Nauheim in Bohemia.

James received no relief from his back pain and returned to America in the fall of 1868. By the summer of 1869 he had completed his medical training at Harvard, but a severe nervous breakdown, followed by a period as a recluse in his father's house, made the practice of medicine seem like an impossibility. James' journals from this time of trouble (1869–71) are full of entries about his morbid fear of the dark, and what he refers to as "that pit of insecurity beneath the surface of life." This neurotic malaise continued until that inspirational moment, the discovery of Charles Renouvier's essays.

From this abandonment of psychic determinism and the embracing of what he called an "open" rather than blocked universe stem most of James' important later discoveries in psychology and philosophy.

In the spring of 1872, James' former chemistry teacher, Charles W. Eliot, had become president of Harvard. Eliot offered James a lectureship in comparative anatomy and physiology which he held from 1872 to 1876.

With success in teaching and research (James had established the first experimental psychology lab in America) his psychosomatic back pain disappeared. It is also in this period James developed, independently of C.G. Lange, the James-Lange theory of emotions: emotions should be understood as feelings accompanying bodily changes stimulated by the "perception of exciting objects." This insight, as well as many other original psychophysical theories became the heart of James' *The Principles of Psychology*. In 1878, a few months after James began his happy marriage to Alice Howe Gibbens, the psychologist promised the publisher Henry Holt the manuscript would be delivered within the year. It took over a decade of work and much prodding from Holt to meet the final publication deadline of 1890.

In the closing decade of the 19th century, *The Principles of Psychology* had the same kind of influence on the burgeoning social sciences that the encyclopedia had for the French philosophes of the late 18th century. James' work, published originally in two volumes, summarized and clarified contemporary knowledge in the entire field of psychology. It also systematically presented for the first time James' functionalist approach to the study of the mind. His view, which stressed the practical and experimental over the metaphysical and theoretical, became the dominant point of view in psychology at the time.

In the 1890s William James' attention turned from the psychology lab to religion and ethics. Seven years after *The Principles, The Will to Believe* was published by Longmans and Green in New York. In these years James had thought a great deal about the existence and attributes of God, the problem of free will and determinism, the nature and foundations of ethics, and the possibility of survival after death.

In *The Will to Believe* James, echoing Renouvier and Pascal,[2] advocated the deliberate choice of belief in free will, immortality and God for therapeutic as well as moral reasons.

James suggested faith in these matters is both permissible and reasonable when we face a situation where our choice or option is forced, lively and momentous. A forced option occurs when, in trying to avoid a decision, we have one made for us. A lively option is one that is both psychologically and physically possible. A momentous option is one in which a great deal depends upon what belief we hold. It is clear that one of James' first forced, lively and momentous options was to posit a belief in free will after reading the essay by Renouvier. James' philosophical defense of belief in free will, God, and immortality rested very heavily on this early experience. For James, metaphysical claims were not merely exercises of the intellect, but also decisions that must have great impact on the way our lives unfold. Later critics of James' philosophy of religion have branded his point of view "a theology of wishful thinking,"[3] but *The Will to Believe* is still read as the best example of a well argued voluntarist theory of faith since Blaise Pascal.

By the turn of the century, William James had begun to combine his psychological insights with the metaphysical issues that had occupied his imagination in the 1890s. The result was a classic work in the psychology of religion, *The Varieties of Religious Experience*, given at Edinburgh University in 1901–02 as the Gifford Lectures.

In this work James offers the definition of religion as "the belief that there is an unseen order, and that our supreme good lies in harmoniously adjusting ourselves thereto."[4] He also provides a salient set of necessary and sufficient conditions for a mystical experience, and points out that although there is no real empirical evidence for immortality and the existence of God, they are both hinted at by the inner desire of human beings for help in times of crisis.

During the first years of the 20th century, James' attention turned from religion to philosophy. As a youth in Germany he had studied the perennial philosophical questions by reading Kant, Hegel and Schopenhauer. But by now, James' mind had a decidedly American bent. He soon became attracted to the pragmatic philosophy of C.S. Peirce.[5] In James' hands, pragmatism became a method for judging truth by looking for the practical consequences of an idea. The psychologist turned philosopher put it this way:

> Pragmatism, on the other hand, asks its usual question, 'Grant an idea or belief to be true,' it says, 'what concrete difference will its being true make in anyone's actual life? How will the truth be realized? What experiences will be different from those which would obtain if the belief were

false? What, in short, is the truth's cash value in experiential terms?"[6]

James' philosophical lectures at the Lowell Institute in 1906 and at Columbia University the following year were collected and published under the title *Pragmatism: A New Name for Old Ways of Thinking*. In this work, as well as the Hibbert Lectures delivered at Oxford in 1908–09, James applied his pragmatic theory of truth to a whole range of philosophical issues.

James had retired from Harvard in 1907. After stays at Edinburgh, Oxford and Stanford, in the final years of his life he returned to the more metaphysical issues but with a now fully developed pragmatic theory of truth at the heart of his musings. The results of this final work were seen in *A Pluralistic Universe* (1909), and his two posthumous works, *Some Problems of Philosophy* (1911) and *Essays in Radical Empiricism* (1912).[7]

In *A Pluralistic Universe* James rejected a monistic view of God, preferring what he called "ancient pluralism." "Why search for unity in the world," asked James. "Why is one more excellent than forty-three or than two million and ten?" Instead of "universe" James used the term "multiverse." In his view there was not one God, but one god among many forces that shape time and history.[8]

In 1898 William James had suffered a serious heart attack. By 1910, his heart had deteriorated to the point that death was imminent. After a short trip to Germany in the spring, William returned to America with his brother Henry in the summer. On August 26, 1910, William James died at his summer home in Chocorua, New Hampshire. He was survived by Alice Gibbens James and their four children.

II

In the twenty-five years before World War I William James was the most widely read psychologist in the world. From the outbreak of the First World War through the 1950s, however, the work of James was almost entirely neglected by academic psychologists. In the 1960s, particularly in America and France, with the popularity of phenomenology and existential psychology, his work was rediscovered.

Since then, American and European scholars have begun more accurately to chart the influence of William James on the intellectual life of the West. In 1903, John Dewey described *The Principles of Psychology* as the "spiritual progenitor" of his massive and varied philosophical work. Dewey, while at the University of Chicago, had also inspired a far-reaching reform of American education by carrying into social practice central theories of James' functional psychology.

The political and social thought of William James can also be found in Theodore Roosevelt's Progressive Revolt of 1912, as well as Woodrow Wilson's emphasis on progress and the shaping of the modern world. Wilson was at heart a Jamesian pragmatist when he insisted that political and social institutions must adapt to the social and economic exigencies of the day. James' indictment of the McKinley administration's "Phillipine Tangle"[9] seems almost prophetic now in light of our Vietnam experiences and the current sabre rattling in the direction of Nicaragua.

But the clearest application of William James' ideas to the political sphere was made by Franklin D. Roosevelt. Pragmatism supplied the philosophical foundation for the New Deal. Roosevelt assumed the society he wished to shape to be malleable and plastic. He adopted a form of James' "social experiment," and judged the results with a pragmatic eye.

In the 1930s James' thought could also be found echoed in the theories of applied sociologists like Jane Addams and Lillian Weld. Indeed, many of the great early contributors to sociology like the Frenchman Emile Durkheim gave credit to the influence James had on their thought.

American theories of jurisprudence were also substantially affected by Jamesian pragmatism. Against the natural law theories popular in the late 18th and 19th centuries, Justice Oliver Wendell Holmes held that the notion of certainty in the law is an outmoded concept. It must be replaced, he argued vigorously, by a theory of law rooted in history and justified by experience. The law, Holmes pointed out, is always approaching but never quite reaching consistency.

In one of Justice Holmes' most celebrated opinions, he appears to be directly quoting William James' essays on pragmatism when he writes, "The best test of truth is the power of the thought to get itself accepted in the competition of the market."

The insights of William James could also be found in a variety of ways in American literature. Both William and Henry were masters of English prose. But their styles were as different as their lives. Henry was an ascetic, a man who made his art his life. William's style was like his teaching— clear, vigorous, and sprinkled with a good bit of American informality. It is sometimes said of the two brothers, and I think rightly, that Henry was the novelist who wrote like a psychologist, and William was the psychologist who wrote like a novelist.

But beyond these observations about style, William James' influence on literature can also be seen in other important ways. He invented the phrase "the stream of consciousness" in *The Principles of Psychology.* The metaphor was used by him there to describe the flux of the mind, its continuity and yet its continuous change. James puts it this way:

> The rush of thoughts is so headlong that it almost always brings us up at the conclusion before we can arrest it. Or if our purpose is nimble enough and we do arrest it, it ceases forthwith to be itself. As a snowflake crystal caught in the warm hand is no longer a crystal but a drop, so instead of catching the feeling of relation moving to its term, we find we have caught some substantial thing, usually the last word we were pronouncing, statically taken, and with its function, tendency, and particular meaning in the sentence quite evaporated. The attempt at introspective analysis in these cases is in fact like seizing a spinning top to catch its motion, or trying to turn up the gas quickly enough to see how the darkness looks.[10]

In Britain, France and America this expression, "the stream of consciousness," became the name for a genre of the novel associated with Dorothy Richardson, Virginia Woolf, Marcel Proust, James Joyce, and others. After James' *The Principles of Psychology*, for the first time novelists were able to explore and actually represent the process of thought James first called "the twilight region that surrounds the clearly lighted center of experience."

In the area of academic philosophy, William James was the first American thinker to enjoy any kind of European reputation. His most famous philosophical work, *Pragmatism*, remained a classic in epistemology among continental philosophers even after American philosophy had turned to the logical analysis of Bertrand Russell and the Wittgenstein of the *Tractatus*.

From the beginning of the 20th century, William James' general theory of aesthetics has been appropriated by a wide range of theorists of art. What these philosophers of art share is James' astute observation that

> Men have no eye but for those aspects
> of things which they have already been
> taught to discern . . . in poetry and the
> arts someone has to come and tell us
> what aspects we may single out, and
> what effects we may single out, and
> what effects we may admire, before our

aesthetic nature can 'dilate' to its full
extent.[11]

Ironically, this same kind of insight about the
context-dependency of art was made later by
Wittgenstein in his *Lectures and Conversations on
Aesthetics, Psychology, and Religious Belief* at a time
when James' essays on aesthetics were being
virtually ignored.

III

The two essays joined in this volume originally
appeared as separate pieces. "The Energies of
Men" was written for a presidential address
delivered by William James before the American
Philosophical Association meetings at Columbia
University, December 28, 1906.

James was six months from retirement and suffering from angina and other physical discomforts. The address was, nevertheless, delivered in
his usual clear, direct and forceful style. The talk
was published a month later in *The Philosophical
Review.* It was republished in October of 1907 in
the *American Magazine* under the title, "The Powers of Men," though James seems to have preferred the earlier title.

The address is hardly the stuff of which contemporary presidential addresses of the Amer-

ican Philosophical Association are made. It is a home-spun talk, written in conversational tone, but nevertheless full of philosophical and psychological insights. It is also useful to remember it was written by a great thinker who realized he was nearing the end of his life.

In this essay, James suggests that the subliminal consciousness is a storehouse of untapped resources available to the individual who posits an act of the will in desiring to retrieve and exploit those reserves. Along the way, James mentions certain disciplines, like katha yoga and the exercises of Ignatius Loyola, that seem to be effective in releasing these stored energies. In some ways, the address is a forerunner to a variety of religious and quasi-religious movements and self-help programs that began to arise in the late 1960s and continue in various permutations to the present day. But it is important that we not confuse a copy with the original item.

James was adamantly opposed to those who used his theories as a way of promoting a cult of the self. He saw any attempt to use his ideas to establish higher sales, find a short-cut to salvation, radiate charm, or win friends and influence people as a perversion of the true purposes of philosophy and religion, not to mention psychology.

As the essay clearly suggests, the untapped energies of the self should be used for the good of humankind as a whole, a theme he returned to repeatedly in other writings such as "The Moral Equivalent of War."

The other essay in this volume, "The Gospel of Relaxation," originally appeared in *Talks to Teachers: and to Students on Some of Life's Ideals*, published by Henry Holt and Co. in 1899. The book, which included a variety of James' best talks, sold for fifty cents. As he informs us in the opening lines of the address:

> I wish in the following hour to take certain psychological doctrines and show their practical applications to mental hygiene—to the hygiene of American life more particularly.[12]

What follows is a discussion of the now famous James-Lange theory of emotions, and an application of that theory in the treatment and alleviation of certain psychological conditions like anxiety, stress reactions and timidity.

In "The Gospel of Relaxation" James develops the notion of a "psychology of imitation." If we wish to cease being anxious, timid or afraid, we must first act *as if* we are not anxious, timid or afraid. If someone is concerned because of a certain lack of courage or truthfulness, one must first act courageous or tell the truth in order to become that way.

It might well be argued that in the ninety years of depth psychology that have intervened since the writing of *Talks to Teachers* the role the unconscious plays in any theory of emotions should not be underestimated. James also lived in an age before the revolution in neurochemistry had begun, and thus little is said about the role played by neurotransmitters in any full understanding of the emotions. James clearly operated in a much more voluntarist frame of mind than most neo-Freudians and neurobiologists are usually willing to do these days.

Still, in "The Gospel of Relaxation" there is real psychological insight about the nature of the individual psyche, much that, once again, can be found later in the century in existentialists like Jean-Paul Sartre.

But perhaps more importantly, James raises a number of relevant questions—perhaps more relevant today than ever—about the possibility of changing and molding a national character. Given our experiences in Vietnam, with Watergate, the Iran-Contra fiasco, and the proliferation of insider trading scandals, James' observations about the importance of first acting as a nation the way we wish to actually become are, like most of his other insights, as fresh as the day they were written.

The initial idea to reprint *On Vital Reserves* came from the publisher at Chirstian Classics, John McHale. His instincts about the contemporary relevance of these essays, as always, were right on the mark.

While preparing this introduction I profited greatly from discussions about James' philosophy with Sister Virgina Geiger, my colleague at the College of Notre Dame. Dr. Margaret Steinhagan helped me to understand James' influence on John Dewey's philosophy of education. Father Joseph Gallagher and Dr. Leon Wurmser stimulated me in ways I cannot enumerate here to put my views about James and other psychologists and philosophers in the larger context of the history of ideas. To these four scholars and fine friends I am very grateful.

Boxer Day, 1987　　　　　STEPHEN JOHN VICCHIO
Baltimore, Maryland

Notes

1. The diary of William James as quoted in *The Thought and Character of William James* by Ralph Barton Perry (New York: Harper and Row, 1935) p. 121.
2. Cf. Pascal's *Pensées*, no. 223.

3. Cf. Bertrand Russell's comments on James in his *Philosophical Essays* (New York: Simon and Shuster, 1966) pp. 112–130.
4. *The Varieties of Religious Experience* (New York: Random House, Modern Library Edition, 1963) p. 53.
5. James and C.S. Peirce were very good friends. One of the few real arguments they had was over James' use of Peirce's pragmatism. In fact, Peirce was so distressed with James' interpretation of the theory that Peirce changed the name of his point of view from pragmatism to pragmaticism. He thought the new name was so ugly no one would be tempted to appropriate it.
6. *Pragmatism: A New Name for Some Old Ways of Thinking* (New York: Longmans and Green, Co., 1907) p. 3.
7. All three published in New York by Longmans and Green.
8. Cf. David Hume's comments in *The Dialogues Concerning Natural Religion*, part IX.
9. Cf. letter to the editor written by William James and published by the *Boston Evening Transcript*, March 1, 1899.
10. *The Principles of Psychology* (New York: Dover Publications, 1950) vol. I, p. 400.
11. *Ibid.* p. 443.
12. *On Vital Reserves* (New York: Henry Holt and Co.) p. 43.

The Energies
of Men

The Energies
of Men[1]

EVERYONE knows what it is to start a piece
of work, either intellectual or muscular, feeling
stale—or *oold*, as an Adirondack guide once put
it to me. And everybody knows what it is to
"warm up" to his job. The process of warming
up gets particularly striking in the phenomenon
known as "second wind." On usual occasions
we make a practice of stopping an occupation
as soon as we meet the first effective layer (so to
call it) of fatigue. We have then walked, played,
or worked "enough," so we desist. That amount
of fatigue is an efficacious obstruction on this
side of which our usual life is cast. But if an
unusual necessity forces us to press onward, a
surprising thing occurs. The fatigue gets worse
up to a certain critical point, when gradually
or suddenly it passes away, and we are fresher
than before. We have evidently tapped a level
of new energy masked until then by the fatigue-

---

[1]This was the title originally given to the Presidential Address delivered before the American Philosophical Association at Columbia
University, December 28, 1906, and published as there delivered in
the *Philosophical Review* for January, 1907. The address was later published, after slight alteration, in the *American Magazine* for October,
1907, under the title "The Powers of Men." The more popular form
is here reprinted under the title which the author himself preferred.
From "Memories and Studies," Longmans, Green & Co., 1911.

obstacle usually obeyed. There may be layer after layer of this experience. A third and a fourth "wind" may supervene. Mental activity shows the phenomenon as well as physical, and in exceptional cases we may find, beyond the very extremity of fatigue-distress, amounts of ease and power that we never dreamed ourselves to own—sources of strength habitually not taxed at all, because habitually we never push through the obstruction, never pass those early critical points.

For many years I have mused on the phenomenon of second wind, trying to find a physiological theory. It is evident that our organism has stored-up reserves of energy that are ordinarily not called upon, but that may be called upon: deeper and deeper strata of combustible or explosible material, discontinuously arranged, but ready for use by anyone who probes so deep, and repairing themselves by rest as well as do the superficial strata. Most of us continue living unnecessarily near our surface. Our energy-budget is like our nutritive budget. Physiologists say that a man is in "nutritive equilibrium" when day after day he neither gains nor loses weight. But the odd thing is that this condition may obtain on astonishingly different amounts of food. Take a man in nutritive equilibrium, and systematically increase or lessen his rations. In the first case he will begin to gain weight, in the second case to lose it. The change will be greatest on the first day, less on the second, less still on the third; and so on till he has gained all that he will gain, or lost all that he will lose, on that altered diet. He is now in nutritive equilibrium again, but with a new weight; and this neither lessens nor increases because his various combustion-processes have adjusted themselves to the changed dietary. He gets rid, in one way or another, of just as much N, C, H, etc., as he takes in *per diem*.

Just so one can be in what I might call "efficiency-equilibrium" (neither gaining nor losing power when once the equilibrium is reached) on astonishingly different quantities of work, no matter in what direction the work may be measured. It may be physical work, intellectual work, moral work, or spiritual work.

Of course there are limits: the trees don't grow into the sky. But the plain fact remains that men the world over possess amounts of resource which only very exceptional individuals push to their extremes of use. But the very same individual, pushing his energies to their extreme, may in a vast number of cases keep the pace up day after day, and find no "reaction" of a bad sort, so long as decent hygienic conditions are preserved. His more active rate of energizing does not wreck him; for the organism adapts itself, and as the rate of waste augments, augments correspondingly the rate of repair.

I say the *rate* and not the *time* of repair. The busiest man needs no more hours of rest than the idler. Some years ago Professor Patrick, of the Iowa State University, kept three young men awake for four days and nights. When his observations on them were finished, the subjects were permitted to sleep themselves out. All awoke from this sleep completely refreshed, but the one who took longest to restore himself from his long vigil only slept one-third more time than was regular with him.

If my reader will put together these two conceptions, first, that few men live at their maximum of energy, and second, that anyone may be in vital equilibrium at very different rates of energizing, he will find, I think, that a very pretty practical problem of national economy, as well as of individual ethics, opens upon his view. In rough terms, we may say that a man who energizes below his normal maximum fails by just so much to profit by his chance at life; and that a nation filled with such men is inferior to a nation run at higher pressure. The problem is, then, how can men be trained up to their most useful pitch of energy? And how can nations make such training most accessible to all their sons and daughters. This, after all, is only the general problem of education, formulated in slightly different terms.

"Rough" terms, I said just now, because the words "energy" and "maximum" may easily suggest only *quantity* to the reader's mind, whereas in measuring the human energies of which I speak, qualities as well as quantities have to be taken into account. Everyone feels that his total *power* rises when he passes to a higher *qualitative* level of life.

Writing is higher than walking, thinking is higher than writing, deciding higher than thinking, deciding "no" higher than deciding "yes"—at least the man who passes from one of these activities to another will usually say that each later involves a greater element of *inner work* than the earlier ones, even though the total heat given out, or the foot-pounds expended by the organism, may be less. Just how to conceive this inner work physiologically is as yet impossible, but psychologically we all know what the word means. We need a particular spur or effort to start us upon inner work; it tires us to sustain it; and when long sustained, we know how easily we lapse. When I speak of "energizing," and its rates and levels and sources, I mean therefore our inner as well as our outer work.

Let no one think, then, that our problem of individual and national economy is solely that of the maximum of pounds raisable against gravity, the maximum of locomotion, or of agitation of any sort, that human beings can accomplish. That might signify little more than hurrying and jumping about in incoordinated ways; whereas inner work, though it so often reinforces outer work, quite as often means its arrest. To relax, to say to ourselves (with the "new thoughters") "Peace! Be Still!" is sometimes a great achievement of inner work. When I speak of human energizing in general, the reader must therefore understand that sum-total of activities, some outer and some inner, some muscular, some emotional, some moral, some spiritual, of whose waxing and waning in himself he is at all times so well aware. How to keep it at an appreciable maximum? How not to let the level lapse? That is the great problem. But the work of men and women is of innumerable kinds, each kind being, as we say, carried on by a particular faculty; so the great problem splits into two sub-problems, thus:

(1). What are the limits of human faculty in various directions?

(2). By what diversity of means, in the differing types of human beings, may the faculties be stimulated to their best results?

Read in one way, these two questions sound both trivial and familiar: there is a sense in which we have all asked them ever since we were born. Yet *as a methodical programme of scientific inquiry*, I doubt whether they have ever been seriously taken up. If answered fully, almost the whole of mental science and of the science of conduct would find a place under them. I propose, in what follows, to press them on the reader's attention in an informal way.

The first point to agree upon in this enterprise is that *as a rule men habitually use only a small part of the powers which they actually possess and which they might use under appropriate conditions.*

Everyone is familiar with the phenomenon of feeling more or less alive on different days. Everyone knows on any given day that there are energies slumbering in him which the incitements of that day do not call forth, but which he might display if these were greater. Most of us feel as if a sort of cloud weighed upon us, keeping us below our highest notch of clearness in discernment, sureness in reasoning, or firmness in deciding. Compared with what we ought to be, we are only half awake. Our fires are damped, our drafts are checked. We are making use of only a small part of our possible mental and physical resources. In some persons this sense of being cut off from their rightful resources is extreme, and we then get the formidable neurasthenic and psychasthenic conditions, with life grown into one tissue of impossibilities, that so many medical books describe.

Stating the thing broadly, the human individual thus lives usually far within his limits; he possesses powers of various sorts which he habitually fails to use. He energizes below his *maximum*, and he behaves below his *optimum*. In elementary faculty, in coordination, in power of *inhibition* and control, in every conceivable way, his life is contracted like the field of vision of an hysteric subject—but with less excuse, for the poor hysteric is diseased, while in the rest of us it is only an inveterate *habit*—the habit of inferiority to our full self—that is bad.

Admit so much, then, and admit also that the charge of being inferior to their full self is far truer of some men than of others; then the practical question ensues: *to what do the better men owe their escape? and, in the fluctuations which all men feel in their own degree of energizing, to what are the improvements due, when they occur?*

In general terms the answer is plain:

Either some unusual stimulus fills them with emotional excitement, or some unusual idea of necessity induces them to make an extra effort of will. *Excitements, ideas, and efforts,* in a word, are what carry us over the dam.

In those "hyperesthetic" conditions which chronic invalidism so often brings in its train, the dam has changed its normal place. The slightest functional exercise gives a distress which the patient yields to and stops. In such cases of "habit-neurosis" a new range of power often comes in consequence of the "bullying-treatment," of efforts which the doctor obliges the patient, much against his will, to make. First comes the very extremity of distress, then follows unexpected relief. There seems no doubt that *we are each and all of us to some extent victims of habit-neurosis*. We have to admit the wider potential range and the habitually narrow actual use. We live subject to arrest by degrees of fatigue which we have come only from habit to obey. Most of us may learn to push the barrier farther off, and to live in perfect comfort on much higher levels of power.

Country people and city people, as a class, illustrate this difference. The rapid rate of life, the number of decisions in an hour, the many things to keep account of, in a busy city man's or woman's life, seem monstrous to a country brother. He doesn't see how we live at all. A day in New York or Chicago fills him with terror. The danger and noise make it appear like a permanent earthquake. But *settle* him there, and in a year or two he will have caught the pulse-beat. He will vibrate to the city's rhythms; and if he

only succeeds in his avocation, whatever that
may be, he will find a joy in all the hurry and
the tension, he will keep the pace as well as any
of us, and get as much out of himself in any
week as he ever did in ten weeks in the country.

The stimuli of those who successfully respond
and undergo the transformation here, are duty,
the example of others, and crowd-pressure and
contagion. The transformation, moreover, is a
chronic one: the new level of energy becomes
permanent. The duties of new offices of trust are
constantly producing this effect on the human
beings appointed to them. The physiologists
call a stimulus "dynamogenic" when it increases
the muscular contractions of men to whom it
is applied; but appeals can be dynamogenic
morally as well as muscularly. We are witnessing
here in America today the dynamogenic effect of
a very exalted political office upon the energies
of an individual who had already manifested a
healthy amount of energy before the office came.

Humbler examples show perhaps still better
what chronic effects duty's appeal may produce
in chosen individuals. John Stuart Mill somewhere says that women excel men in the power
of keeping up sustained moral excitement. Every case of illness nursed by wife or mother is
a proof of this; and where can one find greater

examples of sustained endurance than in those
thousands of poor homes, where the woman successfully holds the family together and keeps it
going by taking all the thought and doing all
the work—nursing, teaching, cooking, washing,
sewing, scrubbing, saving, helping neighbors,
"choring" outside—where does the catalogue
end? If she does a bit of scolding now and then
who can blame her? But often she does just the
reverse; keeping the children clean and the man
good tempered, and soothing and smoothing the
whole neighborhood into finer shape.

Eighty years ago a certain Montyon left to the
Académie Française a sum of money to be given
in small prizes to the best examples of "virtue"
of the year. The academy's committees, with
great good sense, have shown a partiality to
virtues simple and chronic, rather than to her
spasmodic and dramatic flights; and the exem-
plary housewives reported on have been won-
derful and admirable enough. In Paul Bourget's
report for this year we find numerous cases,
of which this is a type; Jeanne Chaix, eldest of
six children, mother insane, father chronically
ill. Jeanne, with no money but her wages at a
pasteboard-box factory, directs the household,
brings up the children, and successfully main-
tains the family of eight, which thus subsists,
morally as well as materially, by the sole force
of her valiant will. In some of these French cases

charity to outsiders is added to the inner family burden; or helpless relatives, young or old, are adopted, as if the strength were inexhaustible and ample for every appeal. Details are too long to quote here; but human nature, responding to the call of duty, appears nowhere sublimer than in the person of these humble heroines of family life.

Turning from more chronic to acuter proofs of human nature's reserves of power, we find that the stimuli that carry us over the usually effective dam are most often the classic emotional ones, love, anger, crowd-contagion or despair. Despair lames most people, but it wakes others fully up. Every siege or shipwreck or polar expedition brings out some hero who keeps the whole company in heart. Last year there was a terrible colliery explosion at Courrières in France. Two hundred corpses, if I remember rightly, were exhumed. After twenty days of excavation, the rescuers heard a voice. *Me voici,*" said the first man unearthed. He proved to be a collier named Nemy, who had taken command of thirteen others in the darkness, disciplined them and cheered them, and brought them out alive. Hardly any of them could see or speak or walk when brought into the day. Five days later, a different type of vital endurance was unexpectedly unburied in the person of one Berton who, isolated from any but dead companions, had been able to sleep away most of his time.

A new position of responsibility will usually show a man to be a far stronger creature than was supposed. Cromwell's and Grant's careers are the stock examples of how war will wake a man up. I owe to Professor C. E. Norton, my colleague, the permission to print part of a private letter from Colonel Baird-Smith written shortly after the six weeks' siege of Delhi, in 1857, for the victorious issue of which that excellent officer was chiefly to be thanked. He writes as follows:

". . . My poor wife had some reason to think that war and disease between them had left very little of a husband to take under nursing when she got him again. An attack of camp-scurvy had filled my mouth with sores, shaken every joint in my body, and covered me all over with sores and livid spots, so that I was marvellously unlovely to look upon. A smart knock on the ankle-joint from the splinter of a shell that burst in my face, in itself a mere *bagatelle* of a wound, had been of necessity neglected under the pressing and incessant calls upon me, and had grown worse and worse till the whole foot below the ankle became a black mass and seemed to threaten mortification. I insisted, however, on being allowed to use it till the place was taken, mortification or no; and though the pain was sometimes horrible, I carried my point and kept up to the last. On the day after the assault I had an unlucky fall on some bad ground, and it was an open question for a day or two whether I hadn't broken my arm at the elbow. Fortunately it turned out to be only a severe sprain, but I am still conscious of the wrench it gave me. To crown the whole pleasant catalogue, I was worn to a shadow by a constant diarrhoea, and consumed as much opium as would have done credit to my father-in-law [Thomas De Quincey]. However, thank God, I have a good share of Tapleyism in me and come out strong under difficulties. I think I may confidently say that no man ever saw me out of heart, or ever heard one croaking word from me even when our prospects were gloomiest. We were sadly scourged by the cholera, and it was almost appalling to me to find that out of twenty-seven officers present, I could only muster fifteen for the operations of the attack. However, it was done, and after it was done came the collapse. Don't be horrified when I tell you that for the whole of the actual siege, and in truth for some little time before, I almost lived on brandy. Appetite for food I had none, but I forced myself to eat just sufficient to sustain life, and I had an incessant craving for brandy as the strongest stimulant I could get. Strange to say, I was quite unconscious of its affecting me in the slightest degree. *The excitement of the work was so great that no lesser one seemed to have any chance against it, and I certainly never found my intellect clearer or my nerves stronger in my life.* It was only my wretched body that was weak, and the moment the real work was done by our becoming complete masters of Delhi, I broke down without delay and discovered that if I wished to live I must continue no longer the system that had kept me up until the crisis was passed. With it passed away as if in a moment all desire to stimulate, and a perfect loathing of my late staff of life took possession of me."

Such experiences show how profound is the alteration in the manner in which, under excitement, our organism will sometimes perform its physiological work. The processes of repair become different when the reserves have to be used, and for weeks and months the deeper use may go on.

Morbid cases, here as elsewhere, lay the normal machinery bare. In the first number of Dr. Morton Prince's *Journal of Abnormal Psychology*, Dr. Janet has discussed five cases of morbid impulse, with an explanation that is precious for my present point of view. One is a girl who eats, eats, eats, all day. Another walks, walks, walks, and gets her food from an automobile that escorts her. Another is a dipsomaniac. A fourth pulls out her hair. A fifth wounds her flesh and burns her skin. Hitherto such freaks of impulse

have received Greek names (as bulimia, dromo-
mania, etc.) and been scientifically disposed of
as "episodic syndromata of hereditary degen-
eration." But it turns out that Janet's cases are
all what he calls psychasthenics, or victims of a
chronic sense of weakness, torpor, lethargy, fatigue, insufficiency, impossibility, unreality, and
powerlessness of will; and that in each and all of
them the particular activity pursued, deleterious
though it be, has the temporary result of raising
the sense of vitality and making the patient feel
alive again. These things reanimate: they would
reanimate *us*, but it happens that in each patient
the particular freak-activity chosen is the only
thing that does reanimate; and therein lies the
morbid state. The way to treat such persons is to
discover to them more usual and useful ways of
throwing their stores of vital energy into gear.

Colonel Baird-Smith, needing to draw on alto-
gether extraordinary stores of energy, found that
brandy and opium were ways of throwing them
into gear.

Such cases are humanly typical. We are all to
some degree oppressed, unfree. We don't come
to our own. It is there, but we don't get at it.
The threshold must be made to shift. Then many
of us find that an eccentric activity—a "spree,"
say—relieves.

There is no doubt that to some men sprees and excesses of almost any kind are medicinal, temporarily at any rate, in spite of what the moralists and doctors say.

But when the normal tasks and stimulations of life don't put a man's deeper levels of energy on tap, and he requires distinctly deleterious excitements, his constitution verges on the abnormal. The normal opener of deeper and deeper levels of energy is the will. The difficulty is to use it, to make the effort which the word volition implies. But if we *do* make it (or if a god, though he were only the god Chance, makes it through us), it will act dynamogenically on us for a month. It is notorious that a single successful effort of moral volition, such as saying "no" to some habitual temptation, or performing some courageous act, will launch a man on a higher level of energy for days and weeks, will give him a new range of power. "In the act of uncorking the whiskey bottle which I had brought home to get drunk upon," said a man to me, "I suddenly found myself running out into the garden, where I smashed it on the ground. I felt so happy and uplifted after this act, that for two months I wasn't tempted to touch a drop."

The emotions and excitements due to usual situations are the usual inciters of the will. But these act discontinuously; and in the intervals the shallower levels of life tend to close in and shut us off. Accordingly, the best practical knowers of the human soul have invented the thing known as methodical ascetic discipline to keep the deeper levels constantly in reach. Beginning with easy tasks, passing to harder ones, and exercising day by day, it is, I believe, admitted that disciples of asceticism can reach very high levels of freedom and power of will.

Ignatius Loyola's spiritual exercises must have produced this result in innumerable devotees. But the most venerable ascetic system, and the one whose results have the most voluminous experimental corroboration, is undoubtedly the Yoga system in Hindustan. From time immemorial, by Hatha Yoga, Raja Yoga, Karma Yoga, or whatever code of practice it might be, Hindu aspirants to perfection have trained themselves, month in and out, for years. The result claimed, and certainly in many cases accorded by impartial judges, is strength of character, personal power, unshakability of soul. In an article in the *Philosophical Review*,[2] from which I am largely copying here, I have quoted at great length the experience with "Hatha Yoga" of a very gifted European friend of mine who, by persistently carrying out for several months its methods

---

[2] "The Energies of Men." *Philosophical Review*, vol. xvi, No. 1, January, 1907. [Cf. Note on p. 3.]

of fasting from food and sleep, its exercises in breathing and thought-concentration, and its fantastic posture-gymnastics, seems to have succeeded in waking up deeper and deeper levels of will and moral and intellectual power in himself, and to have escaped from a decidedly menacing brain-condition of the "circular" type, from which he had suffered for years.

Judging by my friend's letters, of which the last I have is written fourteen months after the Yoga training began, there can be no doubt of his relative regeneration. He has undergone material trials with indifference, travelled third-class on Mediterranean steamers, and fourth-class on African trains, living with the poorest Arabs and sharing their unaccustomed food, all with equanimity. His devotion to certain interests has been put to heavy strain, and nothing is more remarkable to me than the changed moral tone with which he reports the situation. A profound modification has unquestionably occurred in the running of his mental machinery. The gearing has changed, and his will is available otherwise than it was.

My friend is a man of very peculiar temperament. Few of us would have had the will to start upon the Yoga training, which, once started, seemed to conjure the further will power needed out of itself. And not all of those who could launch themselves would have reached the same results. The Hindus themselves admit that in some men the results may come without call or bell. My friend writes to me: "You are quite right in thinking that religious crises, love-crises, indignation-crises may awaken in a very short time powers similar to those reached by years of patient Yoga-practice."

Probably most medical men would treat this individual's case as one of what it is fashionable now to call by the name of "self-suggestion," or "expectant attention"—as if those phrases were explanatory, or meant more than the fact that certain men can be influenced, while others cannot be influenced, by certain sorts of *ideas*. This leads me to say a word about ideas considered as dynamogenic agents, or stimuli for unlocking what would otherwise be unused reservoirs of individual power.

One thing that ideas do is to contradict other ideas and keep us from believing them. An idea that thus negates a first idea may itself in turn be negated by a third idea, and the first idea may thus regain its natural influence over our belief and determine our behavior. Our philosophic and religious development proceeds thus by credulities, negations, and negating of negations.

But whether for arousing or for stopping belief,
ideas may fail to be efficacious, just as a wire
at one time alive with electricity may at another
time be dead. Here our insight into causes
fails us, and we can only note results in general
terms. In general, whether a given idea shall be
a live idea depends more on the person into
whose mind it is injected than on the idea itself. Which is the suggestive idea for this person, and which for that one? Mr. Fletcher's disciples regenerate themselves by the idea (and the
fact) that they are chewing, and rechewing, and
super-chewing their food. Dr. Dewey's pupils
regenerate themselves by going without their
breakfast—a fact, but also an ascetic idea. Not
everyone can use *these* ideas with the same success.

But apart from such individually varying sus-
ceptibilities, there are common lines along which
men simply as men tend to be inflammable by
ideas. As certain objects naturally awaken love,
anger, or cupidity, so certain ideas naturally
awaken the energies of loyalty, courage, endurance, or devotion. When these ideas are effective in an individual's life, their effect is often
very great indeed. They may transfigure it, unlocking innumerable powers which, but for the
idea, would never have come into play. "Father-
land," "the Flag," "the Union," "Holy Church,"
"the Monroe Doctrine," "Truth," "Science," "Liberty," Garibaldi's phrase, "Rome or Death," etc.,

are so many examples of energy-releasing ideas.
The social nature of such phrases is an essential
factor of their dynamic power. They are forces of
detent in situations in which no other force pro-
duces equivalent effects, and each is a force of
detent only in a specific group of men.

The memory that an oath or vow has been made
will nerve one to abstinences and efforts otherwise impossible; witness the "pledge" in the
history of the temperance movement. A mere
promise to his sweetheart will clean up a youth's
life all over—at any rate for a time. For such effects an educated susceptibility is required. The
idea of one's "honor," for example, unlocks energy only in those of us who have had the education of a "gentleman," so called.

That delightful being, Prince Pueckler-Muskau,
writes to his wife from England that he has invented "a sort of artificial resolution respecting
things that are difficult of performance. My de-
vice," he continues, "is this: *I give my word of honor
most solemnly to myself* to do or to leave undone
this or that. I am of course extremely cautious
in the use of this expedient, but when once the
word is given, even though I afterwards think I
have been precipitate or mistaken, I hold it to be
perfectly irrevocable, whatever inconveniences I
foresee likely to result. If I were capable of breaking my word after such mature consideration,
I should lose all respect for myself—and what

man of sense would not prefer death to such an alternative? . . . When the mysterious formula is pronounced, no alteration in my own view, nothing short of physical impossibilities, must, for the welfare of my soul, alter my will. . . . I find something very satisfactory in the thought that man has the power of framing such props and weapons out of the most trivial materials, indeed out of nothing, merely by the force of his will, which thereby truly deserves the name of omnipotent."[3]

Conversions, whether they be political, scientific, philosophic, or religious, form another way in which bound energies are let loose. They unify us, and put a stop to ancient mental interferences. The result is freedom, and often a great enlargement of power. A belief that thus settles upon an individual always acts as a challenge to his will. But, for the particular challenge to operate, he must be the right challeng*ee*. In religious conversions we have so fine an adjustment that the idea may be in the mind of the challengee for years before it exerts effects; and why it should do so then is often so far from obvious that the event is taken for a miracle of grace, and not a natural occurrence. Whatever it is, it may be a highwater mark of energy, in which "noes," once impossible, are easy, and in which a new range of "yeses" gains the right of way.

---

[3]"Tour in England, Ireland, and France," Philadelphia, 1833, p. 435.

We are just now witnessing a very copious
unlocking of energies by ideas in the persons
of those converts to "New Thought," "Christian Science," "Metaphysical Healing," or other
forms of spiritual philosophy, who are so numerous among us today. The ideas here are
healthy-minded and optimistic; and it is quite
obvious that a wave of religious activity, anal-
ogous in some respects to the spread of early
Christianity, Buddhism, and Mohammedanism,
is passing over our American world. The common feature of these optimistic faiths is that
they all tend to the suppression of what Mr. Horace Fletcher calls "fearthought." Fearthought
he defines as the "self-suggestion of inferiority"; so that one may say that these systems
all operate by the suggestion of power. And
the power, small or great, comes in various
shapes to the individual—power, as he will tell
you, not to "mind" things that used to vex him,
power to concentrate his mind, good cheer, good
temper—in short, to put it mildly, a firmer, more
elastic moral tone.

The most genuinely saintly person I have ever
known is a friend of mine now suffering from
cancer of the breast—I hope that she may par-
don my citing her here as an example of what
ideas can do. Her ideas have kept her a practically well woman for months after she should
have given up and gone to bed. They have an-
nulled all pain and weakness and given her a

cheerful active life, unusually beneficent to others to whom she has afforded help. Her doctors, acquiescing in results they could not understand, have had the good sense to let her go her own way.

How far the mind-cure movement is destined to extend its influence, or what intellectual modifications it may yet undergo, no one can foretell. It is essentially a religious movement, and to academically nurtured minds its utterances are tasteless and often grotesque enough. It also incurs the natural enmity of medical politicians, and of the whole trades-union wing of that profession. But no unprejudiced observer can fail to recognize its importance as a social phenomenon today, and the higher medical minds are already trying to interpret it fairly, and make its power available for their own therapeutic ends.

Dr. Thomas Hyslop, of the great West Riding Asylum in England, said last year to the British Medical Association that the best sleep-producing agent which his practice had revealed to him, was *prayer*. I say this, he added (I am sorry here that I must quote from memory), purely as a medical man. The exercise of prayer, in those who habitually exert it, must be regarded by us doctors as the most adequate and normal of all the pacifiers of the mind and calmers of the nerves.

But in few of us are functions not tied up by the exercise of other functions. Relatively few medical men and scientific men, I fancy, can pray. Few can carry on any living commerce with "God." Yet many of us are well aware of how much freer and abler our lives would be were such important forms of energizing not sealed up by the critical atmosphere in which we have been reared. There are in everyone potential forms of activity that actually are shunted out from use. Part of the imperfect vitality under which we labor can thus be easily explained. One part of our mind dams up—even *damns* up!—the other parts.

Conscience makes cowards of us all. Social conventions prevent us from telling the truth after the fashion of the heroes and heroines of Bernard Shaw. We all know persons who are models of excellence, but who belong to the extreme philistine type of mind. So deadly is their intellectual respectability that we can't converse about certain subjects at all, can't let our minds play over them, can't even mention them in their presence. I have numbered among my dearest friends persons thus inhibited intellectually, with whom I would gladly have been able to talk freely about certain interests of mine, certain authors, say, as Bernard Shaw, Chesterton, Edward Carpenter, H. G. Wells, but it wouldn't do, it made them too uncomfortable, they wouldn't play, I had to be silent. An intellect thus tied down by literality and decorum makes on one the same sort of an impression that an able-bodied man would who should habituate himself to do his work with only one of his fingers, locking up the rest of his organism and leaving it unused.

I trust that by this time I have said enough to convince the reader both of the truth and of the importance of my thesis. The two questions, first, that of the possible extent of our powers; and, second, that of the various avenues of approach to them, the various keys for unlocking them in diverse individuals, dominate the whole problem of individual and national education. We need a topography of the limits of human power, similar to the chart which oculists use of the field of human vision. We need also a study of the various types of human being with reference to the different ways in which their energy-reserves may be appealed to and set loose. Biographies and individual experiences of every kind may be drawn upon for evidence here.[4]

---

[4]"This would be an absolutely concrete study . . . The limits of power must be limits that have been realized in actual persons, and the various ways of unlocking the reserves of power must have been exemplified in individual lives. . . . So here is a program of concrete individual psychology. . . . It is replete with interesting facts, and points to practical issues superior in importance to anything we know." *From the Address as originally delivered before the Philosophical Association; see xvi, Philosophical Review, 1, 19.*

The Gospel of
Relaxation

The Gospel of Relaxation[1]

I WISH in the following hour to take certain psychological doctrines and show their practical applications to mental hygiene—to the hygiene of our American life more particularly. Our people, especially in academic circles, are turning towards psychology nowadays with great expectations; and, if psychology is to justify them, it must be by showing fruits in the pedagogic and therapeutic lines.

The reader may possibly have heard of a peculiar theory of the emotions, commonly referred to in psychological literature as the Lange-James theory. According to this theory, our emotions are mainly due to those organic stirrings that are aroused in us in a reflex way by the stimulus of the exciting object or situation. An emotion of fear, for example, or surprise, is not a direct effect of the object's pressure on the mind, but an effect of that still earlier effect, the bodily commotion which the object suddenly excites; so that, were this bodily commotion suppressed, we should not so much *feel* fear as call the sit-

---

[1] From "Talks to Teachers on Psychology: and to Students on Some of Life's Ideas," Henry Holt and Company, 1899.

uation fearful; we should not feel surprise, but coldly recognize that the object was indeed astonishing. One enthusiast has even gone so far as to say that when we feel sorry it is because we weep, when we feel afraid it is because we run away, and not conversely. Some of you may perhaps be acquainted with the paradoxical formula. Now, whatever exaggeration may possibly lurk in this account of our emotions (and I doubt myself whether the exaggeration be very great), it is certain that the main core of it is true, and that the mere giving way to tears, for example, or to the outward expression of an anger-fit, will result for the moment in making the inner grief or anger more acutely felt. There is, accordingly, no better known or more generally useful precept in the moral training of youth, or in one's personal self-discipline, than that which bids us pay primary attention to what we do and express, and not to care too much for what we feel. If we only check a cowardly impulse in time, for example, or if we only *don't* strike the blow or rip out with the complaining or insulting word that we shall regret as long as we live, our feelings themselves will presently be the calmer and better, with no particular guidance from us on their own account. Action seems to follow feeling, but really action and feeling go together; and by regulating the action, which is under the more direct control of the will, we can indirectly regulate the feeling, which is not.

Thus the sovereign voluntary path to cheerfulness, if our spontaneous cheerfulness be lost, is
to sit up cheerfully, to look round cheerfully, and
to act and speak as if cheerfulness were already
there. If such conduct does not make you soon
feel cheerful, nothing else on that occasion can.
So to feel brave, act as if we *were* brave, use all
our will to that end, and a courage-fit will very
likely replace the fit of fear. Again, in order to
feel kindly toward a person to whom we have
been inimical, the only way is more or less delib-
erately to smile, to make sympathetic inquiries,
and to force ourselves to say genial things. One
hearty laugh together will bring enemies into a
closer communion of heart than hours spent on
both sides in inward wrestling with the mental
demon of uncharitable feeling. To wrestle with
a bad feeling only pins our attention on it, and
keeps it still fastened in the mind: whereas, if
we act as if from some better feeling, the old
bad feeling soon folds its tent like an Arab, and
silently steals away.

The best manuals of religious devotion accordingly reiterate the maxim that we must let our
feelings go, and pay no regard to them whatever. In an admirable and widely successful little
book called "The Christian's Secret of a Happy
Life," by Mrs. Hannah Whithall Smith, I find this
lesson on almost every page. *Act* faithfully, and
you really have faith, no matter how cold and

even how dubious you may feel. "It is your purpose God looks at," writes Mrs. Smith, "not your feelings about that purpose; and your purpose, or will, is therefore the only thing you need attend to. . . . Let your emotions come or let them go, just as God pleases, and make no account of them either way. . . . They really have nothing to do with the matter. They are not the indicators of your spiritual state, but are merely the indicators of your temperament or of your present physical condition."

But you all know these facts already, so I need no longer press them on your attention. From our acts and from our attitudes ceaseless inpouring currents of sensation come, which help to determine from moment to moment what our inner states shall be: that is a fundamental law of psychology which I will therefore proceed to assume.

A Viennese neurologist of considerable reputation has recently written about the *Binnenleben*, as he terms it, or buried life of human beings. No doctor, this writer says, can get into really profitable relations with a nervous patient until he gets some sense of what the patient's *Binnenleben* is, of the sort of unuttered inner atmosphere in which his consciousness dwells alone with the secrets of its prison-house. This inner personal tone is what we can't communicate or describe articulately to others; but the wraith and ghost of it, so to speak, are often what our friends and intimates feel as our most characteristic quality. In the unhealthy-minded, apart from all sorts of old regrets, ambitions checked by shames and aspirations obstructed by timidities, it consists mainly of bodily discomforts not distinctly localized by the sufferer, but breeding a general self-mistrust and sense that things are not as they should be with him. Half the thirst for alcohol that exists in the world exists simply because alcohol acts as a temporary anaesthetic and effacer to all these morbid feelings that never ought to be in a human being at all. In the healthy-minded, on the contrary, there are no fears or shames to discover; and the sensations that pour in from the organism only help to swell the general vital sense of security and readiness for anything that may turn up.

Consider, for example, the effects of a well-toned *motor-apparatus*, nervous and muscular, on our general personal self-consciousness, the sense of elasticity and efficiency that results. They tell us that in Norway the life of the women has lately been entirely revolutionized by the new order of muscular feelings with which the use of the *ski*, or long snow-shoes, as a sport for both sexes, has made the women acquainted. Fifteen years ago the Norwegian women were even more than the women of other lands votaries of the old-fashioned ideal of femininity, "the domestic angel," the "gentle and refining influence" sort of thing. Now these sedentary fireside tabby-cats of Norway have been trained, they say, by the snow-shoes into lithe and audacious creatures, for whom no night is too dark or height too giddy, and who are not only saying goodby to the traditional feminine pallor and delicacy of constitution, but actually taking the lead in every educational and social reform. I cannot but think that the tennis and tramping and skating habits and the bicycle craze which are so rapidly extending among our dear sisters and daughters in this country are going also to lead to a sounder and heartier moral tone, which will send its tonic breath through all our American life.

I hope that here in America more and more the ideal of the well-trained and vigorous body will be maintained neck by neck with that of the well-trained and vigorous mind as the two co-equal halves of the higher education for men and women alike. The strength of the British Empire lies in the strength of character of the individual Englishman, taken all alone by himself. And that strength, I am persuaded, is perennially nourished and kept up by nothing so much as by the national worship, in which all classes meet, of athletic outdoor life and sport.

I recollect, years ago, reading a certain work by
an American doctor on hygiene and the laws
of life and the type of future humanity. I have
forgotten its author's name and its title, but I
remember well an awful prophecy that it con-
tained about the future of our muscular system.
Human perfection, the writer said, means abil-
ity to cope with the environment; but the environment will more and more require mental
power from us, and less and less will ask for
bare brute strength. Wars will cease, machines
will do all our heavy work, man will become
more and more a mere director of nature's energies, and less and less an exerter of energy on
his own account. So that, if the *homo sapiens* of
the future can only digest his food and think,
what need will he have of well-developed muscles at all? And why, pursued this writer, should
we not even now be satisfied with a more del-
icate and intellectual type of beauty than that
which pleased our ancestors? Nay, I have heard
a fanciful friend make a still further advance in
this "new-man" direction. With our future food,
he says, itself prepared in liquid form from the
chemical elements of the atmosphere, pepsi-
nated or half-digested in advance, and sucked up
through a glass tube from a tin can, what need
shall we have of teeth, or stomachs even? They
may go, along with our muscles and our physical courage, while, challenging ever more and
more our proper admiration, will grow the gigan-

tic domes of our crania, arching over our spectacled eyes, and animating our flexible little lips to those floods of learned and ingenious talk which will constitute our most congenial occupation.

I am sure that your flesh creeps at this apocalyptic vision. Mine certainly did so; and I cannot believe that our muscular vigor will ever be a superfluity. Even if the day ever dawns in which it will not be needed for fighting the old heavy battles against Nature, it will still always be needed to furnish the background of sanity, serenity, and cheerfulness to life, to give moral elasticity to our disposition, to round off the wiry edge of our fretfulness, and make us good-humored and easy of approach. Weakness is too apt to be what the doctors call irritable weakness. And that blessed internal peace and confidence, that *acquiescentia in seipso*, as Spinoza used to call it, that wells up from every part of the body of a muscularly well-trained human being, and soaks the indwelling soul of him with satisfaction, is, quite apart from every consideration of its mechanical utility, an element of spiritual hygiene of supreme significance.

And now let me go a step deeper into mental hygiene, and try to enlist your insight and sympathy in a cause which I believe is one of paramount patriotic importance to us Yankees. Many years ago a Scottish medical man, Dr.

Clouston, a mad-doctor as they call him there, or what we should call an asylum physician (the most eminent one in Scotland), visited this country, and said something that has remained in my memory ever since. "You Americans," he said, "wear too much expression on your faces. You are living like an army with all its reserves engaged in action. The duller countenances of the British population betoken a better scheme of life. They suggest stores of reserved nervous force to fall back upon, if any occasion should arise that requires it. This inexcitability, this presence at all times of power not used, I regard," continued Dr. Clouston, "as the great safeguard of our British people. The other thing in you gives me a sense of insecurity, and you ought somehow to tone yourselves down. You really do carry too much expression, you take too intensely the trivial moments of life."

Now Dr. Clouston is a trained reader of the secrets of the soul as expressed upon the countenance, and the observation of his which I quote seems to me to mean a great deal. And all Americans who stay in Europe long enough to get accustomed to the spirit that reigns and expresses itself there, so unexcitable as compared with ours, make a similar observation when they return to their native shores. They find a wild-eyed look upon their compatriots' faces either of too desperate eagerness and anxiety or of too intense

responsiveness and good will. It is hard to say
whether the men or the women show it most.
It is true that we do not all feel about it as Dr.
Clouston felt. Many of us, far from deploring it,
admire it. We say: "What intelligence it shows!
How different from the stolid checks, the codfish eyes, the slow, inanimate demeanor we have
been seeing in the British Isles!" Intensity, ra-
pidity, vivacity of appearance, are indeed with
us something of a nationally accepted ideal; and
the medical notion of "irritable weakness" is not
the first thing suggested by them to our mind,
as it was to Dr. Clouston's. In a weekly paper
not very long ago I remember reading a story in
which, after describing the beauty and interest
of the heroine's personality, the author summed
up her charms by saying that to all who looked
upon her an impression as of "bottled lightning"
was irresistibly conveyed.

Bottled lightning, in truth, is one of our American ideals, even of a young girl's character! Now
it is most ungracious, and it may seem to some
persons unpatriotic, to criticise in public the
physical peculiarities of one's own people, of
one's own family, so to speak. Besides, it may be
said, and said with justice, that there are plenty
of bottled-lightning temperaments in other coun-
tries, and plenty of phlegmatic temperaments
here; and that, when all is said and done, the
more or less of tension about which I am mak-

ing such a fuss is a very small item in the sum total of a nation's life, and not worth solemn treatment at a time when agreeable rather than disagreeable things should be talked about. Well, in one sense the more or less of tension in our faces and in our unused muscles *is* a small thing: not much mechanical work is done by these contractions. But it is not always the material size of a thing that measures its importance: often it is its place and function. One of the most philosophical remarks I ever heard made was by an unlettered workman who was doing some repairs at my house many years ago. "There is very little difference between one man and another," he said, "when you go to the bottom of it. But what little there is, is very important." And the remark certainly applies to this case. The general over-contraction may be small when estimated in foot-pounds, but its importance is immense on account of its *effects on the over-contracted person's spiritual life*. This follows as a necessary consequence from the theory of our emotions to which I made reference at the beginning of this article. For by the sensations that so incessantly pour in from the overtense excited body the overtense and excited habit of mind is kept up; and the sultry, threatening, exhausting, thunderous inner atmosphere never quite clears away. If you never wholly give yourself up to the chair you sit in, but always keep your leg- and body-muscles half contracted for a rise; if you breathe eighteen or nineteen instead of sixteen times a minute, and never quite breathe out at that—what mental mood *can* you be in but one of inner panting and expectancy, and how can the future and its worries possibly forsake your mind? On the other hand, how can they gain admission to your mind if your brow be unruffled, your respiration calm and complete, and your muscles all relaxed?

Now what is the cause of this absence of repose, this bottled-lightning quality in us Americans? The explanation of it that is usually given is that it comes from the extreme dryness of our climate and the acrobatic performances of our thermometer, coupled with the extraordinary progressiveness of our life, the hard work, the railroad speed, the rapid success, and all the other things we know so well by heart. Well, our climate is certainly exciting, but hardly more so than that of many parts of Europe, where nevertheless no bottled-lightning girls are found. And the work done and the pace of life are as extreme in every great capital of Europe as they are here. To me both of these pretended causes are utterly insufficient to explain the facts.

To explain them, we must go not to physical geography, but to psychology and sociology. The latest chapter both in sociology and in psychology to be developed in a manner that approaches adequacy is the chapter on the imitative impulse. First Bagehot, then Tarde, then Royce and Baldwin here, have shown that invention and imitation, taken together, form, one may say, the entire warp and woof of human life, in so far as it is social. The American overtension and jerkiness and breathlessness and intensity and agony of expression are primarily social, and only secondarily physiological, phenomena. They are *bad habits*, nothing more or less, bred of custom and example, born of the imitation of bad models and the cultivation of false personal ideals. How are idioms acquired, how do local peculiarities of phrase and accent come about? Through an accidental example set by some one, which struck the ears of others, and was quoted and copied till at last every one in the locality chimed in. Just so it is with national tricks of vocalization or intonation, with national manners, fashions of movement and gesture, and habitual expressions of face. We, here in America, through following a succession of pattern-setters whom it is now impossible to trace, and through influencing each other in a bad direction, have at last settled down collectively into what, for better or worse, is our own characteristic national type—a type with the production of which, so far as these habits go, the climate and conditions have had practically nothing at all to do.

This type, which we have thus reached by our imitativeness, we now have fixed upon us, for better or worse. Now no type can be *wholly* disadvantageous; but, so far as our type follows the bottled-lightning fashion, it cannot be wholly good. Dr. Clouston was certainly right in thinking that eagerness, breathlessness, and anxiety are not signs of strength: they are signs of weakness and of bad coordination. The even forehead, the slab-like cheek, the codfish eye, may be less interesting for the moment; but they are more promising signs than intense expression is of what we may expect of their possessor in the long run. Your dull, unhurried worker gets over a great deal of ground, because he never goes backward or breaks down. Your intense, convulsive worker breaks down and has bad moods so often that you never know where he may be when you most need his help—he may be having one of his "bad days." We say that so many of our fellow countrymen collapse, and have to be sent abroad to rest their nerves, because they work so hard. I suspect that this is an immense mistake. I suspect that neither the nature nor the amount of our work is accountable for the frequency and severity of our breakdowns, but that their cause lies rather in those absurd feelings of hurry and having no time, in that breathlessness and tension, that anxiety of feature and that solicitude for results, that lack of inner harmony and ease, in short, by which with us the work is so apt to be accompanied, and from which a European who should do the same work would nine times out of ten be free. These perfectly wanton and unnecessary tricks of inner attitude and outer manner in us, caught from the social atmosphere, kept up by tradition, and idealized by many as the admirable way of life, are the last straws that break the American camel's back, the final overflowers of our measure of wear and tear and fatigue.

The voice, for example, in a surprisingly large number of us, has a tired and plaintive sound. Some of us are really tired (for I do not mean absolutely to deny that our climate has a tiring quality); but far more of us are not tired at all, or would not be tired at all unless we had got into a wretched trick of feeling tired, by following the prevalent habits of vocalization and expression. And if talking high and tired, and living excitedly and hurriedly, would only enable us to *do* more by the way, even while breaking us down in the end, it would be different. There would be some compensation, some excuse, for going on so. But the exact reverse is the case. It is your relaxed and easy worker, who is in no hurry, and quite thoughtless most of the while of consequences, who is your efficient worker; and tension and anxiety, and present and future, all mixed up together in our mind at once, are the surest drags upon steady progress and hindrances to our success. My colleague, Professor Munsterberg, an excellent observer, who came here recently, has written some notes on America to German papers. He says in substance that the appearance of unusual energy in America is superficial and illusory, being really due to nothing but the habits of jerkiness and bad coordination for which we have to thank the defective training of our people. I think myself that it is high time for old legends and traditional opinions to be changed; and that, if anyone should begin to write about Yankee inefficiency and feebleness, and inability to do anything with time except to waste it, he would have a very pretty paradoxical little thesis to sustain, with a great many facts to quote, and a great deal of experience to appeal to in its proof.

Well, my friends, if our dear American character is weakened by all this overtension—and I think, whatever reserves you may make, that you will agree as to the main facts—where does the remedy lie? It lies, of course, where lay the origins of the disease. If a vicious fashion and taste are to blame for the thing, the fashion and taste must be changed. And, though it is no small thing to inoculate seventy millions of people with new standards, yet, if there is to be any relief, that will have to be done. We must change ourselves from a race that admires jerk and snap for their own sakes, and looks down upon low voices and quiet ways as dull, to one that, on the contrary,

has calm for its ideal, and for their own sakes
loves harmony, dignity, and ease.

So we go back to the psychology of imitation
again. There is only one way to improve ourselves, and that is by some of us setting an example which the others may pick up and imitate
till the new fashion spreads from east to west.
Some of us are in more favorable positions than
others to set new fashions. Some are much more
striking personally and imitable, so to speak. But
no living person is sunk so low as not to be imitated by somebody. Thackeray somewhere says
of the Irish nation that there never was an Irishman so poor that he didn't have a still poorer
Irishman living at his expense; and, surely, there
is no human being whose example doesn't work
contagiously in *some* particular. The very idiots at
our public institutions imitate each other's peculiarities. And, if you should individually achieve
calmness and harmony in your own person, you
may depend upon it that a wave of imitation will
spread from you, as surely as the circles spread
outward when a stone is dropped into a lake.

Fortunately, we shall not have to be absolute
pioneers. Even now in New York they have
formed a society for the improvement of our national vocalization, and one perceives its machi-
nations already in the shape of various newspa-
per paragraphs intended to stir up dissatisfac-

tion with the awful thing that it is. And, better still than that, because more radical and general, is the gospel of relaxation, as one may call it, preached by Miss Annie Payson Call of Boston, in her admirable little volume called "Power through Repose," a book that ought to be in the hands of every teacher and student in America of either sex. You need only be followers, then, on a path already opened up by others. But of one thing be confident: others still will follow you.

And this brings me to one more application of psychology to practical life, to which I will call attention briefly, and then close. If one's example of easy and calm ways is to be effectively contagious, one feels by instinct that the less voluntarily one aims at getting imitated, the more unconscious one keeps in the matter, the more likely one is to succeed. *Become the imitable thing,* and you may then discharge your minds of all responsibility for the imitation. The laws of social nature will take care of that result. Now the psychological principle on which this precept reposes is a law of very deep and widespread importance in the conduct of our lives, and at the same time a law which we Americans most grievously neglect. Stated technically, the law is this: that *strong feeling about one's self tends to arrest the free association of one's objective ideas and motor processes.* We get the extreme example of this in the mental disease called melancholia.

A melancholic patient is filled through and through with intensely painful emotion about himself. He is threatened, he is guilty, he is doomed, he is annihilated, he is lost. His mind is fixed as if in a cramp on these feelings of his own situation, and in all the books on insanity you may read that the usual varied flow of his thoughts has ceased. His associative processes, to use the technical phrase, are inhibited; and his ideas stand stock-still, shut up to their one monotonous function of reiterating inwardly the fact of the man's desperate estate. And this inhibitive influence is not due to the mere fact that his emotion is *painful.* Joyous emotions about the self also stop the association of our ideas. A saint in ecstasy is as motionless and irresponsive and one-idea'd as a melancholiac. And, without going as far as ecstatic saints, we know how in everyone a great or sudden pleasure may paralyze the flow of thought. Ask young people returning from a party or a spectacle, and all excited about it, what it was. "Oh, it was *fine!* it was *fine!* it was *fine!*" is all the information you are likely to receive until the excitement has calmed down. Probably every one of my hearers has been made temporarily half idiotic by some great success or piece of good fortune. "*Good!* GOOD! GOOD!" is all we can at such times say to ourselves until we smile at our own very foolishness.

Now from all this we can draw an extremely practical conclusion. If, namely, we wish our trains of ideation and volition to be copious and varied and effective, we must form the habit of freeing them from the inhibitive influence of reflection upon them, of egoistic preoccupation about their results. Such a habit, like other habits, can be formed. Prudence and duty and self-regard, emotions of ambition and emotions of anxiety, have, of course, a needful part to play in our lives. But confine them as far as possible to the occasions when you are making your general resolutions and deciding on your plans of campaign, and keep them out of the details. When once a decision is reached and execution is the order of the day, dismiss absolutely all responsibility and care about the outcome. *Unclamp*, in a word, your intellectual and practical machinery, and let it run free; and the service it will do you will be twice as good. Who are the scholars who get "rattled" in the recitation-room? Those who think of the possibilities of failure and feel the great importance of the act. Who are those who do recite well? Often those who are most indifferent. *Their* ideas reel themselves out of their memory of their own accord. Why do we hear the complaint so often that social life in New England is either less rich and expressive or more fatiguing than it is in some other parts of the world? To what is the fact, if fact it be, due unless to the overactive conscience of the people, afraid of either saying something too trivial

and obvious, or something insincere, or something unworthy of one's interlocutor, or something in some way or other not adequate to the
occasion? How can conversation possibly steer
itself through such a sea of responsibilities and
inhibitions as this? On the other hand, conversation does flourish and society is refreshing,
and neither dull on the one hand nor exhausting from its effort on the other, wherever people
forget their scruples and take the brakes off their
hearts, and let their tongues wag as automati-
cally and irresponsibly as they will.

They talk much in pedagogic circles today about
the duty of the teacher to prepare for every lesson in advance. To some extent this is useful. But
we Yankees are assuredly not those to whom
such a general doctrine should be preached. We
are only too careful as it is. The advice I should
give to most teachers would be in the words of
one who is herself an admirable teacher. Prepare
yourself in the *subject so well that it shall be always
on tap:* then in the classroom trust your spon-
taneity and fling away all further care.

My advice to students, especially to girl-
students, would be somewhat similar. Just as
a bicycle chain may be too tight, so may one's
carefulness and conscientiousness be so tense
as to hinder the running of one's mind. Take,
for example, periods when there are many suc-

cessive days of examination impending. One
ounce of good nervous tone in an examination
is worth many pounds of anxious study for it
in advance. If you want really to do your best
in an examination, fling away the book the day
before, say to yourself, "I won't waste another
minute on this miserable thing, and I don't care
an iota whether I succeed or not." Say this sin-
cerely, and feel it, and go out and play, or go to
bed and sleep, and I am sure the results next
day will encourage you to use the method per-
manently. I have heard this advice given to a
student by Miss Call, whose book on muscular
relaxation I quoted a moment ago. In her later
book, entitled "As a Matter of Course," the gospel
of moral relaxation, of dropping things from the
mind, and not "caring," is preached with equal
success. Not only our preachers, but our friends
the theosophists and mind-curers of various
religious sects are also harping on this string.
And with the doctors, the Delsarteans, the various mind-curing sects, and such writers as Mr.
Dresser, Prentice Mulford, Mr. Horace Fletcher,
and Mr. Trine to help, and the whole band of
schoolteachers and magazine readers chiming in,
it really looks as if a good start might be made in
the direction of changing our American mental
habit into something more indifferent and strong.

Worry means always and invariably inhibition
of associations and loss of effective power. Of

course, the sovereign cure for worry is religious faith; and this, of course, you also know. The turbulent billows of the fretful surface leave the deep parts of the ocean undisturbed, and to him who has a hold on vaster and more permanent realities the hourly vicissitudes of his personal destiny seem relatively insignificant things. The really religious person is accordingly unshakable and full of equanimity, and calmly ready for any duty that the day may bring forth. This is charmingly illustrated by a little work with which I recently became acquainted, "The Practice of the Presence of God, the Best Ruler of a Holy Life, by Brother Lawrence, being Conversations and Letters of Nicholas Herman of Lorraine, Translated from the French."[2] I extract a few passages, the conversations being given in indirect discourse. Brother Lawrence was a Carmelite friar, converted at Paris in 1666. "He said that he had been footman to M. Fieubert, the Treasurer, and that he was a great awkward fellow, who broke everything. That he had desired to be received into a monastery, thinking that he would there be made to smart for his awkwardness and the faults he should commit, and so he should sacrifice to God his life, with its pleasures; but that God had disappointed him, he having met with nothing but satisfaction in that state. . . .

---

[2]Fleming H. Revell Company, New York.

"That he had long been troubled in mind from a certain belief that he should be damned; that all the men in the world could not have persuaded him to the contrary; but that he had thus reasoned with himself about it: *I engaged in a religious life only for the love of God, and I have endeavored to act only for Him; whatever becomes of me, whether I be lost or saved, I will always continue to act purely for the love of God. I shall have this good at least, that till death I shall have done all that is in me to love Him.* . . . That since then he had passed his life in perfect liberty and continual joy.

"That when an occasion of practising some virtue offered, he addressed himself to God, saying, 'Lord, I cannot do this unless Thou enablest me'; and that then he received strength more than sufficient. That, when he had failed in his duty, he only confessed his fault, saying to God, 'I shall never do otherwise, if You leave me to myself; it is You who must hinder my failing, and mend what is amiss.' That after this he gave himself no further uneasiness about it.

"That he had been lately sent into Burgundy to buy the provision of wine for the society, which was a very unwelcome task for him, because he had no turn for business, and because he was lame, and could not go about the boat but by rolling himself over the casks. That, however, he gave himself no uneasiness about it, nor about the purchase of the wine. That he said to God, 'It was His business he was about,' and that he afterward found it well performed. That he had been sent into Auvergne, the year before, upon the same account; that he could not tell how the matter passed, but that it proved very well.

"So, likewise, in his business in the kitchen (to which he had naturally a great aversion), having accustomed himself to do everything there for the love of God, and with prayer upon all occasions, for His grace to do his work well, he had found everything easy during fifteen years that he had been employed there.

"That he was very well pleased with the post he was now in, but that he was as ready to quit that as the former, since he was always pleasing himself in every condition, by doing little things for the love of God.

"That the goodness of God assured him He would not forsake him utterly, and that He would give him strength to bear whatever evil He permitted to happen to him; and, therefore, that he feared nothing, and had no occasion to consult with anybody about his state. That, when he had attempted to do it, he had always come away more perplexed."

The simple-heartedness of the good Brother Lawrence, and the relaxation of all unnecessary solicitudes and anxieties in him, is a refreshing spectacle.

The need of feeling responsible all the livelong day has been preached long enough in our New England. Long enough exclusively, at any rate—and long enough to the female sex. What our girl-students and woman-teachers most need nowadays is not the exacerbation, but rather the toning down of their moral tensions. Even now I fear that some one of my fair hearers may be making an undying resolve to become strenuously relaxed, cost what it will, for the remainder of her life. It is needless to say that that is not the way to do it. The way to do it, paradoxical as it may seem, is genuinely not to care whether you are doing it or not. Then possibly, by the grace of God, you may all at once find that you *are* doing it, and, having learned what the trick feels like, you may (again by the grace of God) be enabled to go on.

And that something like this may be the happy experience of all my hearers is, in closing, my most earnest wish.